Science Alive

Forces

Terry Jennings

A⁺

Smart Apple Media

Smart Apple Media is published by Black Rabbit Books
P.O. Box 3263, Mankato, Minnesota 56002

Printed in China

Created by Q2A Media
Series Editor: Honor Head
Book Editor: Katie Dicker
Senior Art Designers: Ashita Murgai, Nishant Mudgal
Designer: Harleen Mehta
Picture Researcher: Poloumi Ghosh
Line Artists: Indernil Ganguly, Rishi Bhardhwaj
Illustrators: Kusum Kala, Sanyogita Lal

Library of Congress Cataloging-in-Publication Data
Jennings, Terry J.
    Forces / Terry Jennings.
    p. cm.—(Smart Apple Media. Science alive)
    Summary: "Explains essential facts about forces and movement, including gravity, friction, pressure, and simple machines. Includes experiments"—Provided by publisher.
    Includes index.
    ISBN 978-1-59920-269-3
    1. Force and energy–Juvenile literature. 2. Power (Mechanics)—Juvenile literature. I. Title.
QC73.4.J455 2009
531'.6—dc22
                                                                            2007049122

All words in **bold** can be found in "Words to Remember" on pages 30–31.

Picture credits
t=top b=bottom c=center l=left r=right m=middle
Cover Images: Main Image: iofoto / Shutterstock   Small Image: Juriah Mosin / Shutterstock:
Picture Partners / Alamy: 4r, Howard Birnstihl/ Photographersdirect: 5, David Madison/ NewSport/ Corbis: 6b,
A. Inden/zefa/ Corbis: 7t, Elena Elisseeva/ Shutterstock: 8, Nasa: 9, Niamh Baldock/ Shutterstock: 12r,
Veer/ Photolibrary: 13, Nick Stubbs/ Shutterstock: 14b, Aleksei K/ Shutterstock: 15, Index Stock / Alamy: 18br,
Charles O'Rear/ CORBIS: 19, CYLU/ Shutterstock: 22b, Alexey Bogdanov/ Shutterstock: 23,
Jim Cummins/ Gettyimages: 24b, Marina Jefferson/ Gettyimages: 25,
Mike Sonnenberg/ Istockphoto: 26br, photoslb/ Shutterstock: 27bl.

9 8 7 6 5 4 3 2 1

Contents

What Are Forces?

Our world is full of things that move. Raindrops fall and cars drive along the road. But what makes them move? The answer is **forces.**

Pushes and Pulls

Everything needs a force to make it move. A force is simply a push or a pull. Whenever you write with a pencil or open a door, for example, you are using a force.

▶ *This girl is using forces to ride a bicycle. She is pushing down on the pedals, and she is also pushing and pulling on the handlebars to steer.*

Different Forces

Forces can be small or large. It takes only a tiny push to move a paper clip, but cars, trucks, and trains do not move unless their engines give them a huge push or pull. When you kick a ball, the force from your foot causes the ball to move. The force from a magnet, however, works without objects touching.

▲ *This **magnet** is pulling steel paper clips toward it.*
Magnetism is a force that works without touching.

Pushes and Pulls

Objects move in the direction in which you push or pull them. However, if an equal force is pushing or pulling in the opposite direction, the object will stay still.

Moving Objects

We usually push an object to move it away from us and pull an object to move it toward us. If the object is heavy, a large push or pull is needed.

◀ *This metal ball is very heavy. The athlete has to push the ball really hard away from his body to move it.*

This sled moves in the direction in which the woman pulls it. If the sled had one child on it, it would be much easier to pull.

◄ This boy's body is pushing down on the chair. The boy does not fall because the strong chair pushes against him with an equal force.

▶ This time, the chair is broken. The boy falls because the force of the chair is too weak to hold him.

Gravity

If you throw a ball high in the air, it will eventually fall back to the ground. This is because of an **invisible** force called **gravity.**

◄ *However high we jump, we always come back down to Earth again. The force of gravity pulls everything towards the center of Earth.*

Gravity and Weight

Gravity makes things feel heavy. If you hang a small weight from an elastic band, the band stretches a little. If you use a larger weight, the band will stretch even more because the pull of gravity on the weight is greater.

▲ *The moon has its own gravity, but because the moon is smaller than the earth, its gravity is weaker. When astronauts walk on the moon, they seem to float between each step because there is less gravity holding them down.*

Try This...

Moon Cycle

Discover why gravity is needed to keep the moon traveling around the earth.

You Will Need
- a tennis ball • string

1 Tie one end of the string around the ball and find a clear area outside.

2 Hold the other end of the string, and swing the ball in a circle above your head. You will find that you have to pull on the string to keep the ball going around.

3 Now let go of the string.

What happened?

When you pull on the string, you are creating a force that keeps the ball moving in a circle. This is like the movement of the moon around the earth—the moon stays close to the earth because it is pulled by the earth's gravity. When you stop this force, the ball stops moving in a circle and flies away.

11

Friction

Sometimes, a rubbing force called **friction** tries to slow us down. Friction stops us from moving quickly, but this force is also very useful.

Sliding Surfaces

Friction is a force between two touching surfaces that try to slide past each other. If both surfaces are rough, there will be a lot of friction.

▶ *This girl is keeping her hands off the slide. This reduces friction so she can slide down quickly.*

Useful Friction

When rough sandpaper is rubbed on wood, the friction causes the wood to wear away and become smoother. Friction can help us stop a bicycle, too. We use the brake blocks to rub against the wheels. The rubber tires also produce good friction against the road to stop the wheels from skidding.

◀ Rock climbers wear special rubber-soled shoes. The soft rubber creates lots of friction against the rock. This keeps them from slipping.

Types of Friction

Air and water can also produce friction. When air and water rub against objects moving through them, they slow down the objects.

Air Resistance

When you ride a bicycle, you can feel the air pushing against you. Racing cyclists wear tight clothes and specially shaped helmets. This helps reduce air **resistance.**

◄ Sometimes air resistance can be useful. Parachutes push against the air as they float down. This makes a parachute move more slowly.

14

Water Resistance

Water also resists objects that try to move through it. Water resistance is even stronger than air resistance. Many sea creatures have **streamlined** bodies to help them move easily through the water.

▲ *Boats have a streamlined shape to reduce friction between the boat and the water. This helps the boat to move faster.*

Try This...

Air Resistance

Find out which shapes create the most air resistance.

You Will Need
• thin cardboard • scissors • a hair dryer • tape

1 Ask an adult to cut two pieces of thin cardboard about 4 inches (10 cm) x 8 inches (20 cm).

2 Fold one piece into a tube with a square-shaped cross section. Fold the other into a tube with an oval-shaped cross section. Secure the cardboard with tape.

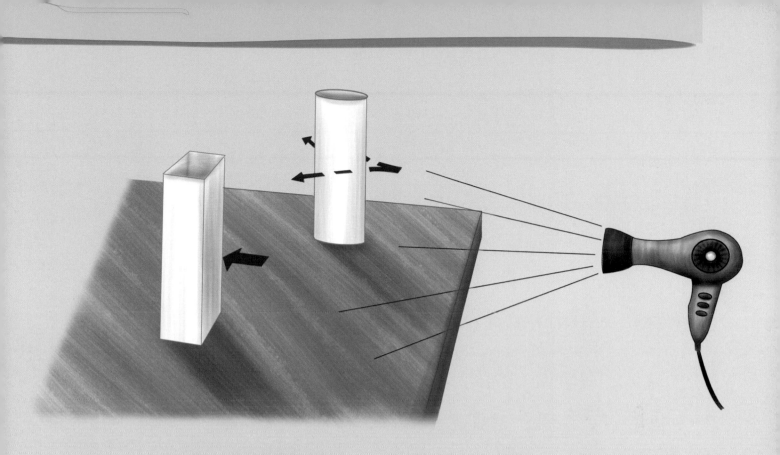

3 Stand the tubes on a desk about 2 inches (5 cm) apart. Ask an adult to help you hold the hair dryer about 3 feet (1 m) from the shapes. Aim a jet of warm air toward them and gradually move the hair dryer forward.

What happened?

The tube with the square-shaped cross section moves back first because it creates the most air resistance. It tries to stop the air pushing against it but is not heavy enough to resist the force. The air moves more easily around the oval-shaped cross section.

Movement

Forces change the way that things move. They can cause objects to start or stop moving or to change speed. Forces can also make objects change shape or direction.

Changing Speed

A large force will make an object move quickly. If an object is moving, and you push hard on it in the direction in which it is moving, it will speed up, or **accelerate.** If the force is in the opposite direction, it will slow down, or **decelerate.**

▶ *Pushing hard on this swing makes it move faster than pushing it gently. Pushing in the same direction as the swing is moving will also make the movement faster.*

Changing Shape

Forces can change the shape of some objects. You can change the shape of modeling clay, for example, by pushing and pulling on it. The bigger the force, the more you can change an object's shape.

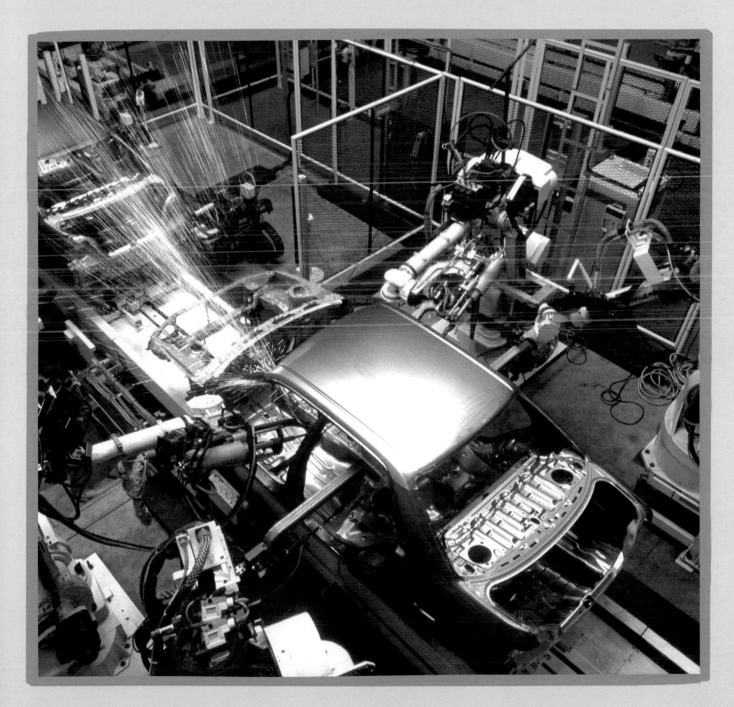

▲ *In this car factory, giant machines have used a lot of force to press steel sheets into the shape of a car.*

Try This...
Moving Objects

Look at how the size of a force affects the movement of an object.

You Will Need
• a piece of thick cardboard about 12 inches (30 cm) x 6 inches (15 cm) • some books
• a small model car

 Place the piece of cardboard on a desk and prop one end up with a book to make a ramp.

2 Place a small model car at the top of the slope. Let the car run down the slope and across the desk.

3 Add another book to make the slope steeper and release the car again. Repeat the experiment with three or four books.

What happened?

Gravity pulls down on the car and makes it travel down the slope. The force of gravity increases when the ramp gets steeper. This causes the car to accelerate. Friction between the car and the table eventually causes the car to slow down and then stop.

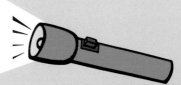

Pressure

When you press or push on something you are adding **pressure.** A bicycle tire is under pressure when you add more air to it, for example.

Pressure and Area

Pressure increases when a large force is added to a small area. If you push a thumb tack against the wall, for example, it will leave a mark. This is because you are applying a force to a small area.

▼ *This digger has sharp teeth. They pass easily into the soil because the force of the digger is applied to a small area.*

Air Pressure

Gravity pulls all the air around the earth down toward the ground. Although air is light, it stretches for hundreds of miles above our heads. We do not notice the huge weight of air pressing down on us because there is pressure in our bodies pushing back.

▲ *Water is heavier than air. When these divers swim underwater, the pressure of the water on their body is greater than that of air.*

Floating

When you put an object in water, the force of the water pushes the object upward. If this push is greater than the object's weight, the object **floats**.

Floating and Sinking

When objects are put in water, they cause the water level to move up. A heavy brick will **sink** in water because it is heavier than the water it pushes aside.

▼ You can feel the force of water pushing up on a beach ball if you try to push it underwater.

Floating in the Air

Air pushes up on objects, too. But this force is so small that we do not notice it. The upward force of air can be seen with very light objects, such as **helium**-filled balloons.

▶ *Helium is a gas that is lighter than the air. When balloons are filled with helium, the upward force of the air causes them to float up.*

Simple Machines

Every day, we use **machines** to help us with tasks. Screwdrivers and wheels are types of machines. They make forces bigger or cause forces to change direction.

The Lever

A **lever** is a long bar that turns around a fixed point. If a small force is added to the long end of the bar, it produces a larger force at the short end.

◀ *A pull on the handle of this hammer causes the other end to move upward, lifting the nail easily.*

The Pulley

A **pulley** is a grooved wheel with a rope running over it. A pulley can change the direction of a force. It is often used for lifting.

▶ *This pulley has two wheels. As the long rope is pulled down, the weight goes up. Pulleys make it easier to lift weights because they spread the force over a longer distance.*

Pulling this rope down lifts the weight up.

Gravity pulls the weight down.

◀ *This crane uses levers and pulleys to lift and move objects around a building site.*

Try This...
Pulley Wheel

Look at how a simple pulley increases the size of a force.

You Will Need
• string • two large metal paper clips • modeling clay

1 Ask an adult to cut three pieces of string, one 3 feet (1 m) long and two 1 foot (30 cm) long. Tie the short strings to the single-loop end of each paper clip.

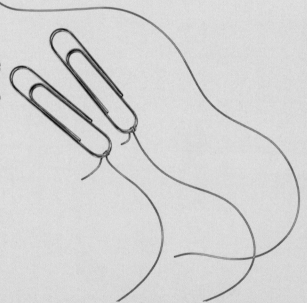

2 Tie one of the paper clips to a door handle so that it hangs down. Put a blob of modeling clay at the end of the string on the other paper clip.

3 Tie the long string to the bottom loop of the hanging paper clip. Pass the string through the loop of the other paper clip, then back through the center loop of the first paper clip.

4 Pull down on the long string to raise the blob of modeling clay.

What happened?

You have made a pulley using paper clips. When you pull down on the long string, the modeling clay moves up. The clay is easy to lift because the pulley spreads the force of your pull over a longer distance.

Words to Remember

Accelerate
To speed up.

Decelerate
To slow down.

Floats
An object floats when it is supported by air or water.

Forces
Pushes or pulls that cause objects to move.

Friction
A rubbing force that tries to stop two surfaces moving against each other.

Gravity
The force that attracts objects toward the center of the earth or other large objects.

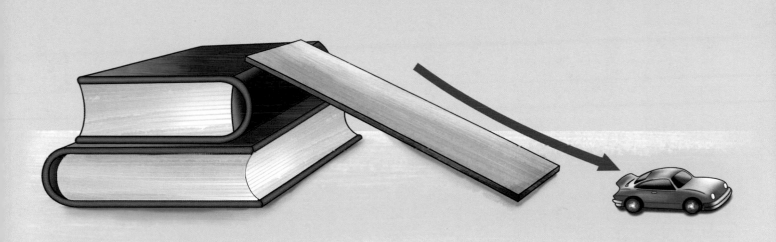

Helium
A type of gas.

Invisible
Something that
you cannot see.

Lever
A long bar that
turns around
a fixed point.
Levers are a
type of machine.

Machines
Devices that help
us to do work
more easily.

Magnet
An object that
attracts metals
such as iron
and steel.

Pressure
A force
pressing down
on an area.

Pulley
A grooved
wheel with a
rope or chain
going over it.

Resistance
A type of friction
that slows down
moving objects.

Sink
An object sinks
when it is heavier
than water.

Streamlined
To have a smooth
shape that passes
easily through
air or water.

Index

Web Finder

For Kids:

http://www.physics4kids.com/files/motion_intro.html

http://pbskids.org/zoom/activities/sci/

http://www.sciencenewsforkids.org/

For Teachers:

http://school.discoveryeducation.com/lessonplans/programs/forces/

http://www.lessonplanspage.com/ScienceLessonFriction.htm

http://www.science-class.net/Physics/Physics.htm